Tips 2 Save

Tips 2 Save

A practical guide to savings, in every aspect of your life,
for financial safety and protection.

By Tom Cashmen and Mary Morrelli

Financial Tips & Strategies saving you money, in an economic global meltdown

Real People
Achieving Real Results

A practical guide to savings, in every aspect of your life, for financial safety and protection.

With the uncertainty of the Banking System, the Federal Government's "bailout" programs, the inability of Banks to lend money and extend credit for any reason, the downsizing of small and large businesses, bankruptcies being at an all time national high (personal and business), the auto makers failing, the airline industry in shambles, employer layoffs on the rise, the uncertainty of any one's job stability, food prices increasing, energy prices rising, and so much more, remember this;

These are challenging times to reduce our debt, get out of debt, control and be better managers of our finances and what we spend. We have been, for the most part, unwise in our spending habits. We need to drastically change those bad habits, immediately, for our financial protection. Let's make wise decisions for our financial future.

Tips 2 Save - Table of Contents

Budgeting

Establishing a monthly budget

Establish a budget for your home, and stick to it

Develop a budget, IN WRITING, with the monthly living expenses, and STAY WITH IT!

So very important in these difficult economic times, to do so. Without a budget, it is financial suicide. There are programs out there to track your budget. Quicken, Quick Books, Peach Tree, to mention a few.

You can also do it on a computer spreadsheet.

TIP: As a part of your budget, include an amount you place in a saving account. Open one, if you don't have one. To save money, you have to consciously write a check to your savings account and DEPOSIT IT!! It may only be $10 per week, but write the check to your savings account.

$10 per week equals $520 per year. Times this for twenty years, at an interest rate of 6% equals approx. $20,000 in savings. $10 adds up dramatically. Could pay 1-2 years of your children's College tuition. If we only knew. Wow. Open that savings account today!!!!!!

4

Budgeted Income & Expenses

Budgeted Income

I/C Category	Budget	Inc/Dec	New Budget	I/C Category	Inc./Dec	Savings	New Budget
W-2 Income				Additional			
Dividend I/C				I/C Lines			
Interest I/C							
Alimony							
Child Support							
Net Rental I/C above exp.							
Home Based Business							
Annuity I/C							
Stock Sales							
Misc. I/C #1							
Misc. I/C #2							
Misc. I/C #3							
Misc. I/c #4							
Total Monthly Income				Total Monthly Income cont...			

Your Budgeted Expenses

Category	Existing Budget	Savings	Reduced Budget	Notes	Category	Existing Budget	Savings	Reduced Budget
Mortgage/Rent					Loans – boat			
Utilities					Loans – Jewelry			
Telephone					Loans – Furniture			
Cell Phone					Other Loans			
Internet					Gasoline			
Home Ins.					Tolls			
Car Repairs					School Supplies			
Health Ins.					Day Care			
Clothing					Tuition			
Food					Travel			
Medical- out of pocket					Entertainment			
Home Repair					IRA/401K			
Lawn Care					Savings			
Life Ins.					Misc. #1			
Car Payments					Misc. #2			
Credit Card Paym'ts					Misc. #3			
Cable								
					Total Expenses			

Budgeted Income and Expenses

Category	Amount	Notes
Net Income Per Month		
Net Reduced Expenses Per Month		
Excess (Shortage) per Month		

Home Owners Insurance

(1) Make sure that you have an "A" rated company

(2) Change your deductible to $500 or $1,000 to save on the premium. The insurance agent won't tell you this.

(3) Have the same insurance company insure your home and your vehicles for insurance savings. There is an economy of scale for the insurance company to have both premiums.

(4) Ask your insurance agent, if your house burned completely down to the ground, would they pay the "replacement value" of the home or something less. If something less, change to replacement value immediately.

(5) Review your contents with your insurance agent for the amount of coverage, and place riders of items that are not specifically covered by your policy. Furs, jewelry, art, antiques, coins, certain furniture

(6) Burn, with a hot iron rod, your name on every electronic item, TV's,

(7) Make a spreadsheet , list, of your assets; asset type,   serial #, manufacturer, supplier, etc. Attach your receipts with this list and place in a safe deposit box in a Bank. If you are robbed, this will insure the reimbursement.

(8) Make a video of each room of your home. This will assist you to recall what was there, and act as a proof to the insurance company, if a theft occurs.

(9) Place your insurance out to bid every two years

Home Heating Costs

(1) Do a review of your house/apartment and identify areas where are leaking out. Around doors, windows, fireplaces, and other "drafty areas".

    (a) Use caulk, weather stripping, door sweeps, plastic, and anything else to close off these leaks.

(2) Minimize the use of ventilation fans in bathrooms and kitchen hood fans in the winter months. These fans can suck the entire heat out of an average house in an hour. This increases your heat cost substantially.

(3) Do not heat areas of the house we don't use regularly, like guest rooms, pantries, and the like. Close the heat vents or turn your thermostat back in those areas, close the doors, and save energy immediately.

(4) Use space heaters, to heat the rooms we spend time in.

(5) Have your furnace, heat pump, or other heat equipment in top operating order. Unclean/dirty filters reduce the efficiency of your furnace substantially.

    (a) an equipment maintenance, quarterly, will insure that efficiency

(6) Wash clothes in cold water as much as possible

(7) Buy a programmable thermostat to raise, or lower, the temperature of your house at preset times. Cooler when not at home. Less energy.

(8) The temperature on your hot water heater, should be approx. 120 degrees.

   (a) If on the dishwasher you can tell, turn the temperature down on the hot water heater.

   (b) If the hot water heater is in an unheated location, open space, basement, etc., wrap it in an insulation blanket. You can get these at the Home Depot's, Lowe's, Hardware stores, etc.

(9) Spending half the time under a hot shower, on cold mornings, can save up to 33% on the hot water bill.

(10) In the winter months, open your blinds on the sunny side of the house; close your curtains on the shady side of the house. If you don't have curtains, consider installing them. Heavy fabrics curtains, with lots of folds, can prevent cold air from seeping in and warm air from seeping out. This will reduce your heating costs.

(11) Set the thermostat for heat on 68 degrees while awake, and 60-65 degrees , while sleeping, or not at home. If you turn the thermostat above this desired temperature, your house will not heat up and quicker. It will only have the furnace work harder, costing more energy.

(12) Turning the temperature too low, below the desired degree setting, can cost you energy also. The contents of the home have to be reheated, in addition to the air.

(13) Purchase energy saving shower heads, to reduce the quantity of hot water being used. Hotels use them all the time. Ever noticed?

   Tip: Using all these energy tips can save you up to 30% on your energy costs.

(14) Schedule with your utility company the budgeted payment plan. This allows you to apply, in your budget schedule (in writing) a constant monthly amount for your utility costs. It permits you to avoid the extremely high costing months, in the year, and levels the monthly cash outlays.

If your budgeted monthly expense is	$400
If you can save, by these tips 20%	
That equals $80 per month or	$960 per year

Start a home based business to save income taxes

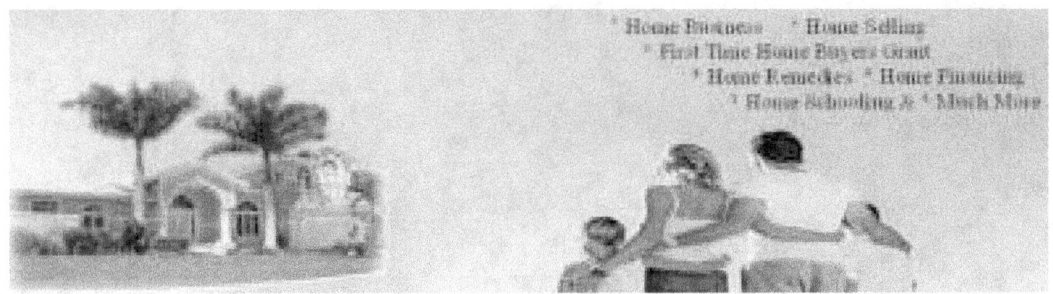

(1) Anyone can start a home based business. Very important to take tax deductions from the same monies that you are spending on gas, repairs, office supplies, home phonecell phone, fax machine, computers, office in the home, utility costs (pro rata), postage, stationery, advertising

(2) A home based business could be your artwork (drawings to sell), knitting, selling your junk in your home online, consulting, typing, auto repair, trash removal, landscaping, grass cutting, and any and all things that you can possibly think of. When you start a home based business you can deduct from your income the expenses in # 1 above, and more.

(3) If you deduct your home based costs of existing funds that you already are spending, like the following; office supplies, your new computer cost, fax machine and supplies, cell phone (business part), home phone (business part), advertising, office in the home and all the related expenses (heat/utilities, homeowners insurance, depreciation on that part of your home %,) , your gas mileage for business travel (at 46.5 cents per business mile (you're already spending the gas anyway), and any other related expenses that you would have for your home business, you will have the following savings;

     (1) Total of business expenses (from #3 above)
     (2) Lets say that they are approximately $4,000
     (3) I will assume that your income on this business is just   ($1,000)
           Net business loss   ($3,000)
     (4) If you are in a 15% Federal tax bracket and
           a 7% State tax bracket that totals 22%   22%
     (5) Minimum amount of tax savings $660

Tip: You are already spending these monies in your monthly budget

Buying a Vehicle

(1) We recommend that you buy a vehicle that is at least 2-3 years old. Depreciation, or value reduction on cars is insane in the first 3 months, and first year, and not good in year two.

(2) When vehicle is purchased in year two or more, the depreciation factor will not be as dramatic, as the first two years.
    (a) Vehicles will drop as much as 40% in the first two years in value.

(3) We do not recommend that you finance a vehicle or anything that has a depreciating value. Jewelry, for the most part, boats (what we refer to as "money pits" in the water), timeshares, TV's, and all the latest state of the art digital equipment on the market, appliances, etc. Pay cash, or don't buy it!!! If you can't afford it don't finance it at 24% with your unfriendly credit card companies. That will even be a greater disaster for you.

(4) Keep your old cars going for as long as possible

Maintaining your old Vehicle

(1) Use common sense.
(2) Change your oil every 3,000 miles. Tune up every 10,000 miles.
(3) Keep proper air pressure in your tires. Keeps gas mileage better for you. When is the last time you checked the air pressure?
(4) Drive the relative speed limit.

    (a) Driving 65 in a 55 m/p/h zone will get you where you are going faster with two problems. (I) you may not get there alive, and get a speeding ticket
    (b) It will reduce your gas mileage approximately 4-5 miles per gallon.

  Savings; Getting optimal gas performance on your vehicle, by maintaining it, driving the elative speed limits can increase your gas efficiency by 5-7 miles per gallon. If you drive 20,000 miles per year, with a vehicle that was getting 18 miles per gallon, that you can increase by 6 miles per gallon will save you approx.

300 gallons of gas per year.
Savings of 300 gallons @ $2 per gallon = $600
    (1) If you have more than one vehicle, multiply the savings by that number of vehicles, at approx. $600 per car.
    (2) Keep your old car going to avoid car payments

(a) Car payments that are $250/ month = per year	$3,000
(b) if repairs to old car = $1,000/year	(1,000)
Net savings per year	$2,000
If it would be a 3 year loan, the total net savings would be	$6,000

(3) Speeding reduces gas mileage and increases gas costs, as already discussed, but increases insurance rates, which will be discussed later in this presentation. Savings could be tremendous, here.

Car and Vehicle Loans

(1) One thing the vehicle loan companies don't want you to know you can make extra payments to your principal balance.

    (a) There is never a "box" on the coupon book for extra principal payments.

    (b) If you are able, make additional principal payments to your vehicle loan to pay down the outstanding balance. Call the lender and get a loan amortization schedule, so you can track your positive progress.

    (c) You can take savings from this seminar and pay down your vehicle principal, but we don't encourage your savings here to be invested in the vehicle loan column.

Automobile Insurance
Reducing Premiums Significantly

(1) Get rid of rental car reimbursement and emergency road side service
    (a) Seldom do you use rental cars for insurance claims. Policies usually pay limited daily amounts, and pay a limited amount for towing charges. (I) Daily rental amounts of $30, and towing is limited to $40, where it costs between $60-$100.
    (b) These premiums add $30-$40 per year to your policy

(2) Remove the uninsured motorist coverage
    (a) This is a double coverage for insurance that you already have. This coverage relates only if the other driver is uninsured.

(3) Remove the medical payment coverage
    (a) This is the same coverage that you have with your life insurance and medical insurance coverage

(4) PIP (Personal Injury Protection) Take the minimum required by your State,
    (a) Have a deductible of $500 - $1,000
    (b) PIP is the same insurance that you already have for hospitalization, employers workers comp, life insurance, etc.

(5) If your car is worth less than $2,500, remove the comprehensive and collision coverage
    (a) In an accident the insurance company only pays you their low assessed value of your vehicle, less any deductible that you have , for any damage or total of the car. $800 value on your car, for the insurance companies sake, with a $2000 repair cost leaves this. The insurance company pays the $800, less your deductible (let's say $500) = $300 to you. Since you will not have much from any accident or repair, exceeding the insurance value, don't pay the high price of the premiums.

(6) Raise your insurance deductible to $500 on the policy
    (a) Comprehensive insurance is damage from fire, theft, breaking into the vehicle illegally. Collision is where your vehicle gets damaged with another vehicle or object accident.
    (b) Raising the deductible from $100 to $500, or even $1,000 will reduce your insurance premiums at least 35% © for out of pocket repairs, etc, below the $500/$1,000 deductible pay yourself.

15

(c) You are not liable for the accident, financially, if it is not your fault.

(d) If your vehicle is financed, the lending company may want a $100 deductible. Make sure that you change that provision to $500

(7) You can add an insurance rider on your vehicle insurance policy inexpensively, for up to $500,000 or even $1,000,000 to cover excess payouts. This coverage may cost you $200 per year.

(8) Property damage - this is coverage that you do to other peoples property, like their fences, shrubbery, house/buildings, etc.

(a) We recommend that you carry property damage up to an amount of $20,000. Do not exceed $40,000. If you have no net worth, or a negative net worth, take the State minimum on this coverage.

Note – Sometimes the vehicle insurance policy will read like 25/40/10. The first two numbers are the bodily injury amounts, $25,000 per person, $40,000 per accident, and the last number is the liability amount. $10,000 per accident.

(9) Bodily Injury Liability – this is a coverage caused by you to another driver, from an accident for your family, people in your car, people in other cars, street pedestrians.

(a) Insure at least your net worth, on this coverage. (I) If your net worth is low, zero, negative , then take the State minimum on this coverage.

(b) Policy limits are expressed in this format; 25/50 = $25,000 per person bodily injury, $50,000 per accident.

(c) Note – your insurance company will provide an attorney for you to settle the others parties claims.

(d) If your net worth is high, cover that amount in this coverage

(e) The bodily injury liability limits appear as follows $10,000/20,000 $15,000/30,000 $20,000/40,000 etc.

Now is the time to put all these cost savings opportunities into practice. The attached spreadsheet will demonstrate the costs savings potential, on correcting your insurance coverage on your vehicle.The first column of the spreadsheet includes the coverage that will be reduced, not needed, or over insured, with an $100 deductible on comprehensive and collision.

Summary of Automobile Savings

Type of Coverage	Premiums Before Changes	Premiums After Changes	Annual Savings	Savings Tip #	Tip	Your Notes
Emergency Road Side Service	15	-0-	15	#1	Remove	
Uninsured Motorist	225	-0-	225	#2	Remove	
Medical Payments	10	-0-	10	#3	Remove	
PIP Personal Injury	60	30	30	$4	State Minimum	
Comprehensive Collision	250	212	38	#5	Raise Deductible to $500 or $1000	
Property Damage	125	108	17	#8	Reduce to Net Worth	
Bodily Injury	300	150	150	#9	Change to $25k/$50K	
Rental Reimbursement	15	-0-	-0-	#1	Remove	
Totals	**$1,000**	**$500**	**$500**			

17

Summary of Automobile Savings (Cont'd)

(1) Don't forget to place your homeowners insurance and vehicle insurance in the same company to save premiums together.

(2) Place your policies out to bid immediately. Insurance companies are in this same difficult financial climate that you are in also, seeking business. If you like a certain insurance carrier, see if they will match another, giving you a lesser rate(s).

(3) A lot of quotes can be compared online, for your coverage.
  (a) Especially after you have adjusted it to the right coverage.

(4) The savings on the prior chart is per car, so multiply the number of cars you insure by the savings amount.

Food Shopping - BIG SAVINGS TIPS

(1) Coupons, coupons, coupons, coupons…

(2) Clip coupons out of every paper, magazine, mailer, and any and all other solicitations, by your food stores, to save large sums of money. You can discount a food purchase, at your store by 15-20%. Adds up. A $200 food bill, discounted 15% = $30

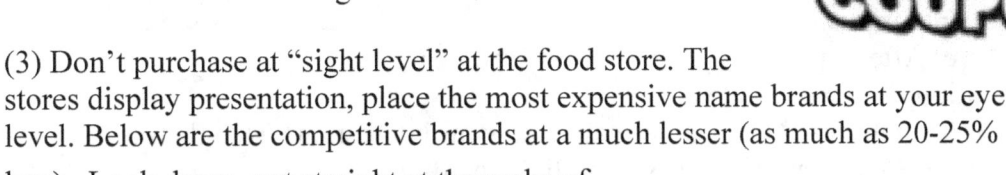

     (a) If you buy food 2 times a month your annual savings will be $720.

(3) Don't purchase at "sight level" at the food store. The stores display presentation, place the most expensive name brands at your eye level. Below are the competitive brands at a much lesser (as much as 20-25% less). Look down, not straight at the racks of

(4) Considering a purchase of a used freezer. A large one. It can be kept in your garage, basement, or any other place in your home.

     (a) Bulk buying is the most advantageous way of purchasing discounted perishable consumer goods.

     (b) Go to large discount food stores, like the Sam's Clubs and others, and purchase large quantities of vegetables, meats, and all other bulk foods that your family will eat.

     (c) Consider buying a side of beef, from a meat slaughter house, farmer, or any other source. This will reduce your meat cost as much as 50%. Store the meat in your purchased freezer.

(5) Tuesdays thru Thursdays are days that the food stores will offer larger discounts, because this is not the heavier times of the shopping week. Food shop on these days.

Credit Card Debt

(1) Do not purchase unless you can pay off, in full, by due date

(2) If you have any debt;

    (a) Take one credit card and pay until you fully pay off. Then pay another credit card, etc. You are then making "progress", rather than spreading small payments over all credit cards, and staying in the hole.

    (b) Note: Making minimum payments on credit cards ill pay off your card in approximately 24 years. What fun while spending at a rate of 20-24%, and giving it to someone else. We all should be so fortunate with our investment returns.

    (c) After paying off your smallest credit card, in full, cut it up and cast it into a fire.

    (d) Credit card Companies can raise your interest rate as high as 30% if you miss one payment. Get away from these cards.

Settling out your credit cards with your Card Companies

(1) Most credit cards can be discounted, with settlements from the credit card companies.

    (a) Do not use a third party company to do so. You don't need them. This can be done yourself.

(2) Here is the method

    (a) Do not pay your credit card for a minimum of 6 months. Here is a projected table of the percentage of settlement an average credit card company will settle with you, on your balance, after time;

Time	% of balance
3-6 months	70%
6-9 months	50-70%
9-12 months	40-60%
12-15 months	30-40%
after 15 months	10-20%

    (b) When you contact them to offer them any settlement amount, make sure you can send the cash immediately. This is the key to success.

Life Insurance

(1) Purchase level term insurance only Like a 20 year level term, where the premiums remain the same over the 20 year period.

(2) Insure enough to take care of your wife, children, for 15-20 years with your current level of income.

(3) Have an irrevocable life insurance trust own your policy, have you as the insured, and the insurance trust becomes the beneficiary. The trust document can spell out the payouts to your wife, children, etc., and the investment vehicles that you want your insurance funds to be placed in. Very important principle here. There are NO income taxes of life insurance proceeds. Yes, only a half truth. There can be estate taxes that can rob your loved ones of the insurance proceeds, and future provision for them. That estate tax could be as high as 50%.

(4) If you have whole life insurance, GET RID OF IT, GET RID OF ITS!!!

(5) Immediately get a 20-30 year level term policy on yourself to give you the same coverage, at a much lesser month/annual premium.

(6) When the level term becomes effective, cancel the whole life policy with a vengeance.

Tip: Remember, it's your money.
> (a) Take the cash value out of the policy and invest into an IRA, (individual retirement account), Roth, Sepp (Self employment pension plan). Invest the funds in a money market account. Not the violent stock market, that is crashing all around us.

Tip: You save money on your level term policy, below the whole life policy. You have a tax deduction for the IRA contribution saving you income taxes.

Tip: Life insurance agents will not tell you that they make more "money" (go figure. it's that "M" word) with a whole life insurance sale , than a level term policy, that will be cheaper for you and your family. It's ironic that money drives their sale, not your best interest. Most insurance agents should have level term policies, not selling the naïve general public the wrong kind of life insurance (whole life) to just fill the linings of their pockets.

21

(7) Purchase level term insurance equal to your outstanding mortgage balance, that will pay off your mortgage upon your death. Place the coverage in the Irrevocable life insurance trust.

Cancel any mortgage insurance that some insurance agent has manipulated you into. It's very expensive insurance, compared to level term insurance. Insurance should be owned, solely, but in an irrevocable insurance trust, never individually.

(8) We don't recommend life insurance on children, but if you need to, purchase $10,000 on each, for burial insurance. Straight level term insurance. It's inexpensive.

Amount of life insurance needed for your family, in your life Insurance trust.
(1) all outstanding debts plus 10 years annual income

Example -		
Yearly "net income " husband/wife		40,000
10 times the net yearly income		$400,000
Debts		
Mortgage	200,000	
Car loans	15,000	
Credit cards	20,000	
other debts	5,000	$240,000
		$640,000

A "Cup" of Coffee can cost you tens of thousands

(1) Going to the local convenient store, 7-11, or wherever to buy your daily caffeine can be a very costly error.

(2) We will say that you just buy a hot drink, not anything else like a bagel, muffin, gum, snacks, etc. and pay the minimum amount for that purchase.

(3) $1.25 times 5 days per week, times 50 weeks per year equals approximately a yearly amount of $300

(4) That is exclusive of any other purchase that you make

(5) Drink your coffee at home, and we will show you how that annual savings, in the grand scheme of our safety net for you will save you over $30,000

Tip: In the morning, prepare your hot beverages at home, and don't buy them out.

Airline Travel Savings

(1) If you have to fly, travel if at all possible, on Tuesdays through Thursdays. These are the least expensive days of the week to travel.

    (a) If you leave on a Tues – Thurs. , stay the weekend, and return on the following Tues – Thurs, if possible: this is the least cost of air travel.

(2) Make your reservations at least two weeks in advance, prior to your flying date. Rates will be approx. 25% less for you here. If at all possible, attempt to make your plans 30 days before departure. You can get some great deals, on the internet, if you do.

(3) Do not use a travel agent. Do it yourself.

(4) Go to different airlines and place your departure and return date in the appropriate boxes. Then you can select the least fares that the airline has to offer. These rates are usually, if not always, less then you can get through calling the reservations agent, of the airline, direct.

(5) After you check your rates, on different airlines websites;

    (a) Go to Travelocity.com and see if there are any better deals for you. There is another website, Cheapfares.com that you may want to compare.

    (b) Oftentimes connecting flights are less expensive than direct non stop flights. Takes longer to travel, but the savings is usually worth it. Is it worth a 3 hour layover to save $180 on your fare? It's saving you $60 per hour to sit. Not bad.

(6) Most times it is significantly less to fly to larger cities of destination, rather than the smaller city, that the airline doesn't service. A rental car, is a rental car, and the drive (with gas) is much less than the flight to the small city.

(7) Airfare from Baltimore, Maryland to Diberville Mississippi. (a smaller city, round trip) $675.

Original Airfare Price	$675
Minus Discount On Air Fare	-$150
Minus Gas, etc…	- $14
Total Price After Savings	$511
Your Savings	**$164**

How To $ave BIG MONEY on Car Rentals

Learn the Secrets They Don't Want You To Know

Tip: Rental cars are least expensive if rented by the week. Even if only need a car for 3 days, the weekly rate may be less expensive. Always have them quote you the weekly rate. Always refuse the additional insurance coverage on the rental car. your own vehicle insurance policy covers you already. Purchasing gas yourself, usually is less expensive then the car rental company will charge you to refill the tank. Sometimes they will charge you 80 cents to $1 more per gallon to fill it for you. Don't let an airline convince you that their rental car affiliate is less expensive. Price this out yourself. The airlines get a commission for this referral.

Saving Money on Your Mortgage

Refinancing your existing mortgage

(1) Consider refinancing your existing mortgage, if the current mortgage interest rate, available on the market, is 2% or less than your current interest rate.

      (a) You can view the interest rates charged by most banks in your local papers, on Sundays. Also the rates are published online, in your area, for the local and national banks.

      (b) When refinancing your mortgage, see if there is a "no fee" refinance, where the lending bank doesn't charge amounts to do this transaction. If they do;

          (i) Verify the total amount of refinance

          (ii) Look at the monthly savings, from the lesser interest rate

          (iii) See how many months of savings it will take you to recoup that amount.

          (iv) We suggest that savings will recoup the fess in less than 24 months. Many lenders will include any fees in the refinance, where you do not have to put any money to do the new loan.

Tip: Financing to a 15 year loan, or buying a new home with a 15 year loan, instead of a 30 year loan

      (1) The actual difference in principal and interest payment between a 30 year mortgage, and a 15 year mortgage at 6.5% , for a loan amount of $200k is approximately $480 per month higher, or 37%.

      (2) We will show the savings for mortgage lengths below a 30 year conventional mortgage term.

Saving Money on Your Mortgage

$200k Mortgage @ 6.5% Interest Rate

# of Years of Your Mortgage	Amount of Monthly Payment	Total Payments over Mortgage Term	Savings Below 30 Year Mortgage	Your Notes	Your Commitment Date
30	$1,264	$455,040	Standard		
25	$1,350	$405,000	$50,040		
20	$1,491	$357,840	$97,200		
15	$1,742	$313,560	$141,480		

27

Saving Money on Your Mortgage

Years of Mortgage	% of Balance Still Due 15 Yr. Mort.	% of Balance Still Due 30 Yr. Mort.		Homeowner's Equity 15 Yr. Mort.	Homeowner's Equity 30 Yr. Mort.
1	97%	99%		3%	1%
2	94	99		6	1
3	90	98		10	2
4	86	97		14	3
5	81	97		19	3
6	76	96		24	4
7	71	95		29	5
8	65	94		35	6
9	58	92		42	8
10	51	91		49	9
11	42	89		58	11
12	33	88		67	12
13	23	86		77	14
14	12	84		88	16
15	-0-	82		100	18

Tip: From the prior chart, the equity that a homeowner has after 10 years of payments on the 15 and 30 year mortgages are:

30 year mortgage	9% equity in your home
15 year mortgage	49% equity in your home

We will quantify that for you:

(1) Assuming your home is worth the same for that 10 year period, hasn't appreciated at all, with a worth of $200,000;

30 year mortgage	$18,000 of equity in your home
15 year mortgage	$98,000 of equity in your home
Difference in equity	$80,000

(1) We will show how to take the savings from this presentation, and apply it to your principal mortgage balance, to save you potentially over $100,000

(2) Making an additional mortgage payment, per year, to your outstanding principal balance.

      (a) This is a powerful principle for mortgage reduction

      (b) One additional payment per year, to reduce directly the outstanding principal balance will reduce these mortgage terms to;

            30 year mortgage to approximately - a 22 year mortgage

            15 year mortgage to approximately - a 11.5 year mortgage

(3) If your mortgage payment, principal and interest is $1,400 per month, make one payment of $1,400 to your principal for the year.

Assumes 200,000 Mortgage, 6.5%, 30 year term making one additional principal payment to Mortgage Balance per year. Saving Money on Your Mortgage

(1) You can even make additional payments on your mortgage, above one principal payment per year.

     (a) In the early years of your mortgage, you can make additional principal payments each month very easily. This requires two things;

          (i) A mortgage amortization schedule, showing the principal amount each month.
          (ii) The financial discipline to pay a little more each month to reduce years from your mortgage debt.

     (b) In these early years, the principal for your mortgage may be as low as $20-$30 per month. Above the extra principal payment, each year to reduce your mortgage term, from the previous slides, pay one or two additional payments of principal per month. It will cost you $40-$60, for two additional principal payments.

     (c) Small amounts add up quick. $40 per month = $480 per year, of additional principal. Reducing two years off a $1,200 per month mortgage saves you $28,800 of mortgage payments.

Great investment!

     (d) Remember, back in a prior page, having that coffee out each day, is spending approximately $300 per year? Place that savings against the principal amount of your mortgage. Home coffee never tasted so good, and never went so far.

Saving Money on your Mortgage
Assumes a $200,000 Mortgage, 6.5%, 30 Year Term
Making one additional principal payment to Mortgage Balance
Per year

Initial Mortgage Term	Reduced Years of Mortgage	Years of Mortgage Reduction	Months Saved	Total Savings
30	22	8	96	$121,344
15	11.5	3.5	41	$71,422

Note:

30 Years   96 months @ $1,264/monthly payment = $121,344

15 Years   41 months @ $1,742/monthly payment = $71,422

31

First Time Buyers

First Time Buyers – there are tremendous benefits available for first time buyers

(1) Low interest rates, from lending institutions
(2) Low or no closing costs, on your purchase
(3) Low or no money down deals
(4) Builders will contribute and pay all your closing costs
(5) There are State Grants available, where you receive a grant from the Federal Government, and or State, to assist in your purchase.
(6) Builders will discount the house, and are desperate to offer great deals, including contributing to closing costs (above) reducing the selling price of the home, offering additional amenities free of charge (tile floors, Korian countertops, upgraded carpet, better windows, etc.)
(7) The tax savings on renting versus buying/owning your home is tremendous.

Saving Money on Your Mortgage
This assumes a $1,200 per month mortgage payment,
or the same in rent Saving Money on Your Mortgage

(1) Don't forget to remove any homeowners life insurance on your home. This was discussed in the life insurance part of this seminar, in previous slides. It is 2-4 times the price of straight level term insurance for a 20 year period.
   (a) Don't forget to place that additional coverage of insurance to pay off your mortgage, in an irrevocable life insurance trust, as previously discussed.
(2) Have your homeowners insurance with your vehicle insurance with the same insurance company, to save monies. That was discussed on a prior slide.
(3) On a new mortgage, be sure to not have any prepayment penalties to pay off the mortgage early. Do not compromise this condition, ever.
(4) Always have a qualified individual review any mortgage before you sign it. $100 to an attorney, for a review, could and probably will save you thousands.
(5) Get a mortgage amortization schedule, from your lender or online, and verify if their principal balance is correct, with your records. Lenders do make mistakes.

32

Saving Money on Your Mortgage

This assumes a $1,200 per month mortgage payment, or the same in rent

Category	Rent	Own	Your Notes
Tax Deduction	None	$14,400	
Appreciation	None	Yes	
Equity	None	Yes	
Tax Savings	None	Yes	
Income tax Savings (Tax bracket = 22%)	None	$3,168	

Determining Your Bad Spending Habits

Keeping track of every penny you spend for 1 month is a great way to figure out your spending weaknesses and bad habits.

Use these itemized forms to keep a record of how you spend your money for the month. Please include all purchases, such as food, clothing, gasoline, bus, subway, or cab fares. Also include payments for bills, such as electric, gas, water, telephone, car and so on.

Keep track of every penny you spend for 1month				
Date	Items	Amount	Need	Not needed

Monthly Spending cont…

Keep track of every penny you spend for 1month				
Date	Items	Amount	Need	Not needed

Monthly Spending cont…

Date	Items	Amount	Need	Not needed
Keep track of every penny you spend for 1month				

Keep track of every penny you spend for 1month				
Date	Items	Amount	Need	Not needed

It's Time To Test Your New Money Spending Habits

Have you become a better monay manager and less bad spending habits

Here is the final test to see how much better you have become at saving your hard earned money.

After you have completed the first Bad Spending Habit 30 Day Tracker, wait 30 days and compare your new spending habits using the following forms. Please include all purchases, such as food, clothing, gasoline, bus, subway, or cab fares. Also include payments for bills, such as electric, gas, water, telephone, car and so on.

Keep track of every penny you spend for 1month				
Date	**Items**	**Amount**	**Need**	**Not needed**

Monthly Spending cont...

Date	Items	Amount	Need	Not needed
Keep track of every penny you spend for 1month				

Monthly Spending cont…

Date	Items	Amount	Need	Not needed
Keep track of every penny you spend for 1month				

Monthly Spending cont…

Date	Items	Amount	Need	Not needed
Keep track of every penny you spend for 1month				

Monthly Spending cont…

Keep track of every penny you spend for 1month				
Date	Items	Amount	Need	Not needed

Personel Goals

1. _____
   _____

2. _____
   _____

3. _____
   _____

4. _____
   _____

5. _____
   _____

Family Members Goals

1. _____
   _____

2. _____
   _____

3. _____
   _____

4. _____
   _____

5. _____
   _____